DISASTER SCIENCE

TSUNAMIS

BY NAOMI CAMERON

Gareth Stevens
PUBLISHING

Please visit our website, www.garethstevens.com. For a free color catalog of all our high-quality books, call toll free 1-800-542-2595 or fax 1-877-542-2596.

Cataloging-in-Publication Data
Names: Cameron, Naomi.
Title: Tsunamis / Naomi Cameron.
Description: Buffalo, NY : Gareth Stevens Publishing, 2027. | Series: Disaster science | Includes glossary and index.
Identifiers: ISBN 9781482482133 (pbk.) | ISBN 9781482482140 (library bound) | ISBN 9781482482157 (ebook)
Subjects: LCSH: Tsunamis--Juvenile literature.
Classification: LCC GC221.5 C364 2027 | DDC 551.4637--dc23

Published in 2027
Gareth Stevens Publishing
2544 Clinton Street
Buffalo, NY 14224

Portions of this work were originally authored by Marne Ventura and published as *Detecting Tsunamis*. All new material in this edition was authored by Naomi Cameron.

Designer: Joshua Olson
Editor: Claire Vanden Branden
Content Consultant: Gerard Fryer, Senior Geophysicist, NOAA Pacific Tsunami Warning Center

Photo Credits: Cover, pp. 1, 15 Frans Delian/Shutterstock.com; p. 4 Thunder Bird, Inc./ Shutterstock.com; p. 6 Falcon video/Shutterstock.com; p. 9 Muralonga/Shutterstock.com; p. 10 David Rydevik/Wikimedia Commons; p. 13 Marisa Estivill/Shutterstock.com; p. 16 Jeff Fox/USGS; p. 19 pedroalmeida103/Shutterstock.com; p. 20 NOAA Photo Library; p. 22 ChameleonsEye/Shutterstock.com; p. 24 Sakarin Sawasdinaka/Shutterstock.com; p. 26 Mirko Kuzmanovic/Shutterstock.com; p. 29 Penguin and Chicken/Shutterstock.com.

Printed in China

CPSIA compliance information: Batch #QS27GS: For further information contact Gareth Stevens at 1-800-542-2595.

TABLE OF CONTENTS

CHAPTER 1

DISASTER IN JAPAN

On March 11, 2011, the seafloor began to shake. Miles below the Pacific Ocean's surface, two **tectonic plates** collided. This caused a massive earthquake. The earthquake started 45 miles (72 km) off the coast of Japan. Shocks could be felt in countries miles away.

It's very common for earthquakes to happen in Japan.

The earthquake triggered a huge tsunami. A giant wave rose nearly 130 feet (40 m) high. Within 30 minutes, it hit Japan. Water skipped over seawalls. Towns were flooded. Water traveled up to 6 miles (10 km) inland in some areas.

The tsunami also hit a nuclear power plant. Three **reactors** exploded. Dangerous **radiation** leaked out. People within 12 miles (20 km) had to **evacuate**.

The tsunami didn't stop there. It spread throughout the Pacific Ocean. Nearly 4,000 miles (6,400 km) away, waves hit the coast of Hawaii. Some were up to 12 feet (3.6 m) high. Nine-foot (2.7-m) waves struck California.

Most of the damage from Japan's 2011 tsunami took place along the coast.

The damage from the tsunami was awful. Some experts estimate that it cost nearly $200 billion in Japan alone. It is thought to be the most expensive natural disaster in history.

WHAT CAUSED THE EARTHQUAKE?

Earth's tectonic plates are constantly moving. This movement is very slow. Japan sits on three of these plates. One of the plates shifted underneath another. As these plates slid against each other, they created a force called friction. This force made one plate stop moving. Eventually, the plates got unstuck. They jolted apart, causing the earthquake. It was the largest earthquake to ever hit Japan.

Boats, cars, and houses were swept away after Japan's 2011 tsunami.

The tragedy caused more than 18,000 deaths. Thousands of people went missing. But many lives were saved, too. A tsunami warning was sent out minutes after the earthquake hit. People in Japan had been trained on what to do. They acted quickly. This saved many lives.

CHAPTER 2

WHAT IS A TSUNAMI?

A tsunami is a series of very long ocean waves. The distance from one **crest** to the next can be as much as 100 miles (160 km). The name *tsunami* comes from the Japanese words *tsu*, meaning "harbor," and *nami*, meaning "waves." Tsunami waves can grow to be as tall as a 10-story building.

A dangerous tsunami hit Thailand in 2004.

Far out at sea, these waves do not usually cause damage or death. But when a tsunami strikes land, it can be incredibly destructive. The waves can sweep away everything in their path.

Sometimes tsunamis are called tidal waves, but they do not come from the normal forces that cause tides. Earthquakes are the most common cause of tsunamis. Earth's crust is made up of plates that are always moving. Sometimes two plates bump into each other and stick. Energy builds up until the plates slip past each other. The energy is released, resulting in an earthquake that rattles the crust. When an earthquake

Cities along coastlines and near earthquake-prone areas are at risk from tsunamis.

happens in the ocean, the movement on the ocean floor **displaces** the water above it. Waves rush outward in the form of a tsunami. Eighty percent of tsunamis follow earthquakes. Rarer causes include volcanoes, landslides, and meteorites.

Tsunamis are dangerous because they happen so fast. People often don't have time to escape the waves. Over the years, people have built many cities along coastlines. Large **populations** are at risk when a tsunami hits. Moving water

HISTORY'S DEADLIEST TSUNAMI

In 2004, a powerful earthquake began near the west coast of the Indonesian island of Sumatra. It triggered an enormous tsunami. Huge waves raced across the Indian Ocean. They struck Thailand, Indonesia, Sri Lanka, and India. More than 230,000 people were killed. Half a million others were injured. It was the deadliest tsunami in recorded history.

The 2004 Indian Ocean tsunami wiped out many communities.

is heavy and powerful. And the danger does not end when the waves settle down. People who survive can have trouble getting food, shelter, and medical help.

RICHARD H. HAGEMEYER
PACIFIC TSUNAMI
WARNING CENTER
NOAA

CHAPTER 3

DETECTING TSUNAMIS

On April 1, 1946, a huge earthquake caused a tsunami that struck Alaska. Waves moved across the ocean to Hawaii, Asia, and the US West Coast. The tsunami killed 159 people.

After this disastrous event, the US government set up the Pacific Tsunami Warning Center, which is based in Hawaii.

The Pacific Tsunami Warning Center is staffed 24 hours a day to monitor for tsunamis.

Scientists there send warnings to Hawaii and island nations in the Pacific Ocean and the Caribbean Sea. The center also monitors areas in the Indian Ocean.

The National Tsunami Warning Center sends warnings to US coastal states and the Canadian coastal provinces. For earthquakes along the US coast, scientists can usually send out warnings within five minutes of the quake being detected. Worldwide, the time is approximately 10 minutes. Scientists are working to bring these times down.

Seismographs are instruments that record where and when earthquakes strike. Scientists use this information

Tide gauges help with monitoring tsunami activity.

to alert people that an underwater earthquake might cause a tsunami. Tide **gauges** measure sea levels. Scientists warn people if a tsunami is on the way to a shoreline.

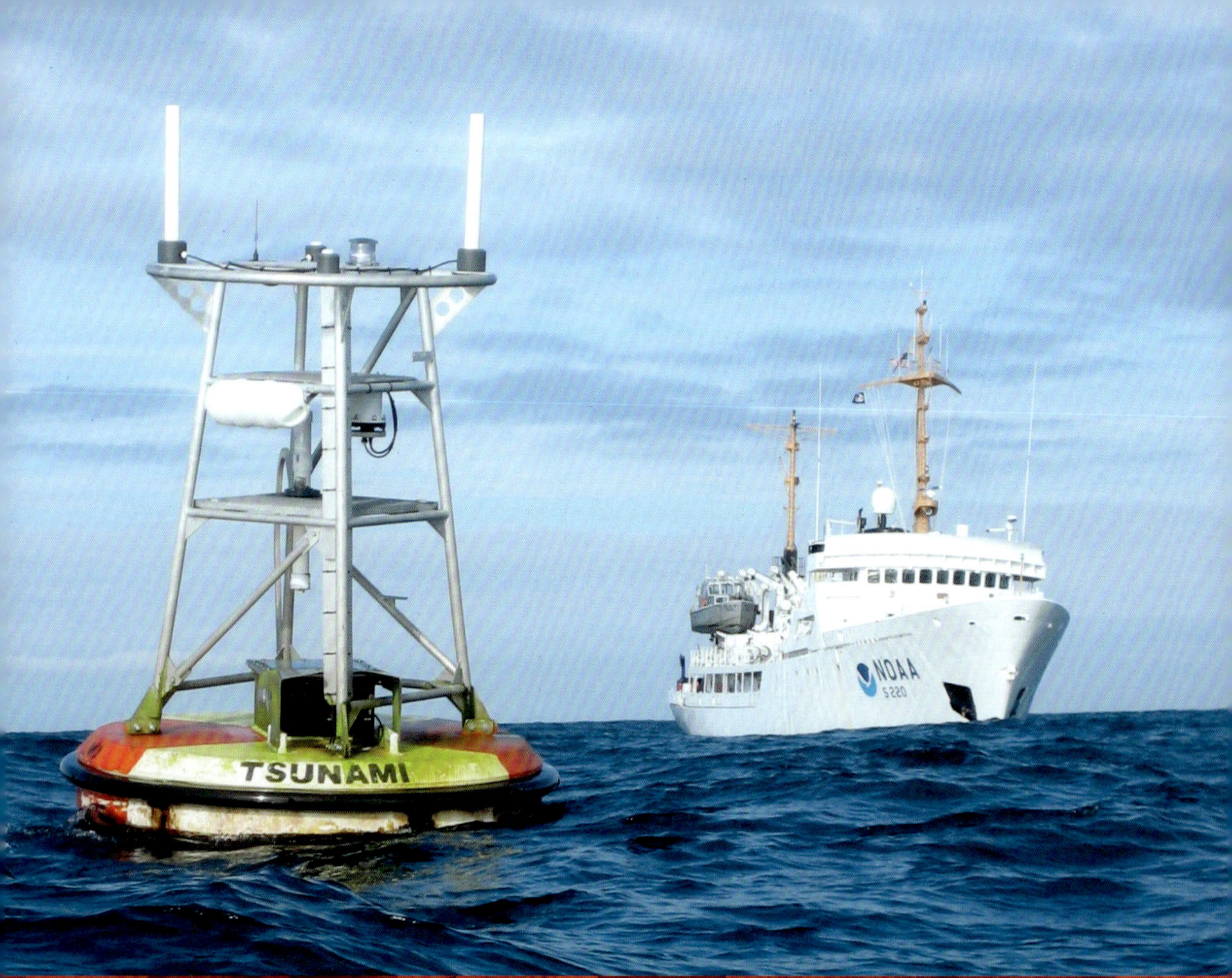

Tsunami warning instruments are placed in the ocean to provide additional warning of approaching waves.

Deep-ocean assessment and reporting of tsunamis (DART) systems are set up on the ocean floor. They measure the sea level. If levels rise, the systems report the data back to scientists. Scientists use this information to help predict where a tsunami might hit. Then they can alert people in those areas.

NOAA

The National Oceanic and Atmospheric Administration (NOAA) is an agency of the US government. Its scientists study the ocean and the atmosphere. They give people information so they can stay safe. The DART program is a part of NOAA. Other countries have their own DART systems, too.

TSUNAMI
HAZARD ZONE
ECO SPIRITS
ecospirits.ch
IN CASE OF A
TSUNAMI ALERT
GO TO HIGH GROUND
OR ASSEMBLY AREA
CD
FAR NORTH DISTRICT COUNCIL
EMERGENCY MANAGEMENT
Far North
District Council

CHAPTER 4

PREPARING FOR A TSUNAMI

When experts send out alerts, they send out a watch or a warning. A tsunami watch means an earthquake has hit the ocean floor. There is a chance a tsunami may strike. A tsunami warning means a tsunami is very likely. It means people must get to safety right away.

Warning signs let people know about local tsunami risks.

In some places, large walls are built to help protect parts of the coastline from tsunamis.

Since 2000, deadly tsunamis have struck Indonesia, Chile, Japan, and Samoa. Leaders in high-risk areas now help people learn about the warning signs of tsunamis. They teach people to get away from the ocean if the water pulls back. They make plans so people know where to go if a wave is coming. They remind people to stay away from the coast for several hours, because tsunamis include a series of waves.

TSUNAMI TYPES

There are different classifications of tsunamis. Local tsunamis wash over coasts within 62 miles (100 km) of the earthquake that caused them. They take an hour or less to hit. Regional tsunamis result from earthquakes between 62 miles (100 km) and 620 miles (1,000 km) away. These take from one to three hours to arrive. Ocean-wide tsunamis can start more than 620 miles (1,000 km) from the shoreline. It takes three or more hours for them to hit. The more time before a tsunami hits, the better the chance there is of sending out warnings so people can get to safety.

In some places, concrete tetrapod blocks are put along shores to help reduce the force of ocean waves.

Specially designed buildings in high-risk areas keep people safer if a tsunami hits. Engineers are finding ways to make buildings stronger. If there isn't time to evacuate, people can move to the top of a building. Japan is in a high-risk area for earthquakes and tsunamis. Engineers there make buildings that absorb shock. During an earthquake or tsunami, these buildings can shift around without breaking.

Scientists still cannot predict when and where a tsunami will hit. But in the past 100 years, they have learned a lot about how tsunamis happen. Advanced technology has allowed them to track these deadly waves. Scientists continue working to find better ways to detect tsunamis and save more lives.

FACT FILE

TSUNAMI SAFETY

If you live in or visit a place where tsunamis are likely, make an evacuation plan with your family. Figure out the safest place to go if a tsunami strikes.

If a tsunami watch is announced, check the radio, TV, or internet to get important updates. If a tsunami warning is announced, immediately get to a safer place on higher ground. Do the same thing if you feel an earthquake near the ocean.

Never go down to the beach to watch a tsunami. Stay as far away from the beach as possible. Remember, tsunamis have more than one wave. The shore can be dangerous for hours.

If you notice an unusual amount of water receding from the shore, this is one sign of a tsunami. Move away from the beach right away.

Signs can help show evacuation routes.

Look for anyone who might need help getting off the beach, such as infants, the elderly, or people with limited mobility. Help them evacuate to safety. Return home only after officials say that your area is safe.

TEST YOUR KNOWLEDGE

Take this quiz to test your knowledge.

1. Summarize Chapter 2 of this book.

2. Do you think sending out a tsunami watch is a good idea? Or should scientists only send out tsunami warnings when a tsunami is very likely to occur? Why?

3. Why do many tsunamis happen in Japan?

- **A.** Earthquakes are common there.
- **B.** The winds are faster there.
- **C.** More meteorites fall there.

4. Which tsunami warning center would tell Californians that a tsunami was going to hit their state?

- **A.** the Pacific Tsunami Warning Center
- **B.** the National Tsunami Warning Center
- **C.** the National Oceanic and Atmospheric Administration

Answers can be found on page 32.

GLOSSARY

crest
The top of an individual wave.

displaces
Moves something out of position.

evacuate
To leave a place of danger.

gauges
Instruments for measuring.

populations
The numbers of people living in particular areas.

radiation
Waves of energy sent out by radioactive material.

reactors
Devices used to produce nuclear energy in power plants.

seismographs
Instruments that measure and record the shaking of the ground.

tectonic plates
Pieces of Earth's crust and upper mantle that form the outer shell of the planet.

FOR MORE INFORMATION

BOOKS

Kerry, Isaac. *Tsunamis*. North Mankato, MN: Pebble, 2022.

Murray, Julie. *Tsunamis*. Minneapolis, MN: Abdo Publishing, 2025.

WEBSITES

Britannica Kids: Tsunami
kids.britannica.com/kids/article/tsunami/400067
Find out more about how and why tsunamis happen.

National Geographic Kids: Tsunami Facts
natgeokids.com/au/discover/geography/physical-geography/tsunamis/
Learn more fascinating facts about tsunamis.

Publisher's note to educators and parents: Our editors have carefully reviewed these websites to ensure that they are suitable for students. Many websites change frequently, however, and we cannot guarantee that a site's future contents will continue to meet our high standards of quality and educational value. Be advised that students should be closely supervised whenever they access the internet.

INDEX

Answer Key: 1. Answers will vary; 2. Answers will vary; 3. A; 4. B